Artist's rendition of mid-nineteenth century map of western
Gouge, 2003. Based on map titled *Europe* (New York: J. H.

Casper *and* Catherine Move to America

Casper and Catherine Move to America

An Immigrant Family's Adventures, 1849–1850

Brian Hasler

Illustrations by Angela M. Gouge

Introduction by Barbara Truesdell
Afterword by M. Teresa Baer

INDIANA HISTORICAL SOCIETY PRESS
INDIANAPOLIS 2003

This book is a publication of the
Indiana Historical Society Press
450 West Ohio Street
Indianapolis, Indiana 46202-3269 USA
www.indianahistory.org
Telephone orders 1-800-447-1830
Fax orders 317-234-0562
Orders by E-mail shop.indianahistory.org

The paper in this publication meets the minimum requirements of American National Standard for Information Sciences—Permanence of Paper for Printed Library Materials, ANSI Z39.48-1984. ∞

Library of Congress Cataloging-in-Publication Data
Hasler, Brian.
  Casper and Catherine move to America : an immigrant family's adventures, 1849–1850 / Brian Hasler ; illustrations by Angela M. Gouge.
    p. cm.
  Summary: Relates the adventures of Casper Hasler, a stonecutter who immigrated to Indiana in 1849, and of his children and wife, Catherine, who remained in Switzerland until their sixth child was born. Includes information about oral history and family history research.
    ISBN 0-87195-168-1
    1. Hasler family—Juvenile literature. 2. Swiss Americans—Biography—Juvenile literature. 3. Immigrants—United States—Biography—Juvenile literature. 4. Pioneers—Indiana—Greene County—Biography—Juvenile literature. 5. Greene County (Ind.)—Biography—Juvenile literature. 6. Switzerland—Emigration and immigration—History—19th century—Juvenile literature. 7. United States—Emigration and immigration—History—19th century—Juvenile literature. [1. Hasler family. 2. Swiss Americans. 3. Immigrants—Indiana. 4. Pioneers—Indiana. 5. Indiana—History—19th century. 6. Oral history. 7. Genealogy.] I. Gouge, Angela M., ill. II. Title.

E184.S9H37 2003
973'.0435—dc21   2003047763

Casper and Catherine Hasler

This book is dedicated with love to my great-great-grandparents,
Casper and Catherine Hasler, who brought our family to America;
to my father, Kenneth Hasler, who shared this story with me
as a small child; and to my son, Hugh Patrick Hasler,
in hopes that he will carry on this family tradition.

Hugh and Kenneth Hasler

Preface

THE EVENTS IN THIS BOOK, which took place more than 150 years ago, are real and tell the story of my family as it was passed down from my father to me. One day, when my son is a little older, I will share our story with him, and our tradition will span six generations.

My ancestors, Casper and Catherine, were true pioneers, leading their family to a better life in America, a new country of opportunity. Their journey from Europe was not easy, and there was much uncertainty about the future when they left Switzerland, the country they had called home. It took courage, faith, and determination to travel to a strange and distant land. What is amazing is that their story is not unusual. America is a nation of immigrants. Your own family may have made the same difficult choices as mine. Whoever your ancestors were, they, too, had to have courage and faith as they started new lives in America.

Every family has stories. Sometimes they are passed down from generation to generation. Often, parts of the story are lost or remembered differently by different family members. Some stories are mysteries that can only be discovered by the careful research of people acting like modern-day detectives.

I hope that in reading the story of my family, children will ask their parents about their own story, and parents will pass on the knowledge they have about their ancestors. Your family story may be more complete than mine, or it may be a mystery to be solved through investigation. Whatever the case, I hope that you will begin your journey today—to learn the story of your family, to write it down for those who follow, and to share it with those you love.

BRIAN HASLER

Introduction
Gathering a Family's Oral History

"The universe is composed of stories, not atoms."
—Muriel Rukeyser

PEOPLE LOVE STORIES. At any family gathering—holidays, family reunions, weddings, or funerals—an important part of the event for everyone is the time spent telling stories about family members. These stories can be funny, sad, exciting, or scary. The stories that a family tells and retells are part of that family's "oral tradition." There may be stories about cousins or grandparents who are known to all the family. There may also be stories about ancestors—family members from the past—who may be remembered only by a few of the oldest relatives or only by the stories still told about them.

The story you are about to read, *Casper and Catherine Move to America*, is about one family's ancestors and their adventures migrating or moving from Europe to America. It is a special form of oral tradition, called a family "legend" or "oral history." This legend is part of the family's story of itself, told in the author's family for generations. By writing it down, the author is preserving it—keeping it alive—for future generations, even if the family forgets to tell the story anymore. Writing it down also makes it possible to share the story with more people. This is important because many families share the experience of migrating from Europe to the United States. By hearing the oral histories of many of these families, we can begin to picture in our minds the larger story of how Europeans became Americans.

Oral history is quite an old way of remembering the past. For thousands of years groups of people passed down their history through storytellers—individuals who memorized stories about their ancestors and created stories about present-day events to tell at gatherings throughout the year.

Older storytellers taught younger storytellers so that the group's history would not be lost. Native American groups passed down their histories this way. Their stories told how the tribes came to America, about the connections between people and nature, about their warriors' brave deeds, and many other things. Today many Native-American stories can be found in books, so that we can all learn from them, but most important, so that the history of Native Americans will continue to be passed down.

When the true stories about people are written down it is called "history," and people who write history are called historians. During the twentieth century oral history became important to American historians as they tried to discover more about our past. They came to realize that oral history often tells about the lives of ordinary people. The stories help historians write history that is about all of us, not just a few "important" people. Today many historians worldwide use both written records and oral traditions, if they are available, in order to create and pass down more complete histories about people. Oral history is especially useful for studying groups that have no written history, for writing biographies—stories about one individual—and for family histories—stories about a family.

However, people do not always remember things exactly as they happened. A living person is not a computer, after all. People have feelings and opinions that help them decide how to tell their stories—what details to share and what details to change. For instance, if your ancestor was a Civil War hero who later turned into a thief, you might be proud to tell other people about his war adventures, but you might not want to tell how he was later sent to jail.

People forget details, too. Stories tend to change over time as a storyteller's memory fades and as a story is repeated by different people. The words change and parts of the story can be added or left out. There are even times when relatives argue about parts of the story! This does not mean the story is untrue—just that some parts may not be entirely correct. As an example, think of the story you are about to read, the story of a Swiss family who moved to Indiana in 1849 to 1850. Some of the minor ideas in the

story probably changed as it was passed down from the author's great-great-grandfather to his great-grandfather to his grandfather to his father to him. But we know that this family really did come to America with seven children! After reading the story, a section called the "Afterword" will tell you how we know that many of the other details of the story are true as well.

Of course, the experiences that happen to us are only part of our lives. Our experiences—and the thoughts and feelings we have about those experiences—help to shape who we are, how we think about ourselves, and how we remember the past. The people around us in our families, neighborhoods, churches, schools, and cities also help to shape who we are, what we think and feel, and how we remember the past. The stories that we share come from what we remember and from what the people around us remember. Our stories help us to see the roads that our own lives have taken and they show us the paths that our families and communities have traveled over time. They can also help us to decide on new courses for our lives.

Everybody has stories to tell. Stories like *Casper and Catherine Move to America* can tell you about a family's history. They can also tell you what the storyteller or the family considers important enough to pass on to future generations—what they value and what they want people to remember about them. You see, oral history is a way to capture a piece of a person's life in his or her own words. This gives us a glimpse into the human heart that we can preserve and pass down for the future.

BARBARA TRUESDELL
Indiana University, Center for the Study of History and Memory

Casper and Catherine Move to America

NE DAY IN SCHOOL, Hugh's teacher, Ms. Thomas, introduced a new boy to the class. His name was Juan, and he had moved with his family to the United States from Costa Rica.

"Juan and his family are immigrants to our country," explained Ms. Thomas. "We are a nation of immigrants. All of our families came to this country from somewhere else—even the Native Americans."

When Hugh was at home that evening, he told his dad, "We have a new boy in class. He's from another country."

"Our family came from another country, too," replied Hugh's dad.

"Ms. Thomas told us about immigrants in school today," Hugh said. "Where did our family come from?"

"Well, sit next to me and I'll tell you a special story," said Hugh's dad. "It's the story of your great-great-great-grandfather and great-great-great-grandmother and the children they brought with them to America."

CASPER AND CATHERINE HASLER lived in the mountains of Switzerland in a town called Bönigen. Casper worked as a stonecutter, and Catherine tended their small farm. Before long, Casper and Catherine had several children: Elizabeth, Louisa, Rudolph, Mary, and Ferdinand—what was considered a *small* family in those days. Their time was filled with hard work and laughter, and they dreamed of a better life ahead for their children.

But times were hard in Switzerland and all over Europe. By 1849 Casper and Catherine saw their life's savings slipping away. Some families were going to America to build a new life in the land of opportunity. After much thought, they decided Casper would go to America alone and prepare a home. Catherine, who was expecting their sixth child, and the other children would join him when they had saved enough money. Bidding his family goodbye, Casper set out for the port city of Hamburg, in one of the northern German states, in order to book passage across the Atlantic Ocean.

Casper was sad to leave Catherine and the children behind; he didn't know when he would see them again. But he was also hopeful for a better life in the future. Hoisting a knapsack filled with crackers over his shoulder and carrying a barrel of cheese under his arm, Casper boarded the sailing ship that would take him to a new country.

On the voyage across the sea, Casper listened to the stories, hopes, and dreams of the other passengers. He heard people speak in strange languages and sing songs he had never heard before. They shared what food they had brought, and Casper traded crackers and cheese for carrots and dried meat. But they shared more than food—they shared the adventure of their journey across the ocean and their plans for new lives in America.

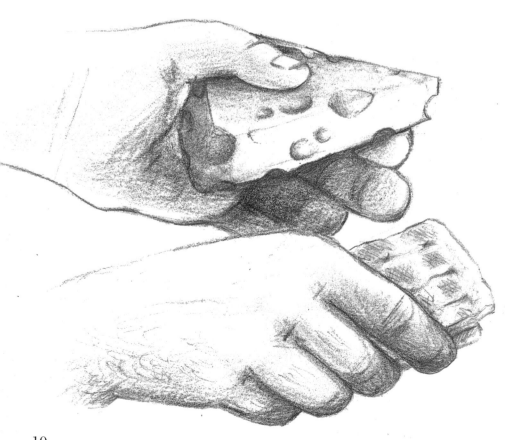

Once in the United States, Casper traveled to Greene County, Indiana. He had heard rumors that Swiss families had settled there, but when he arrived all he heard was the strange language called English. After searching for someone he might understand, he heard his native language, German, being spoken by a man behind him. Casper was so happy to hear his own language that he hugged the man in the middle of the street! This is how Casper made his first friend in America, Mr. Kendrick.

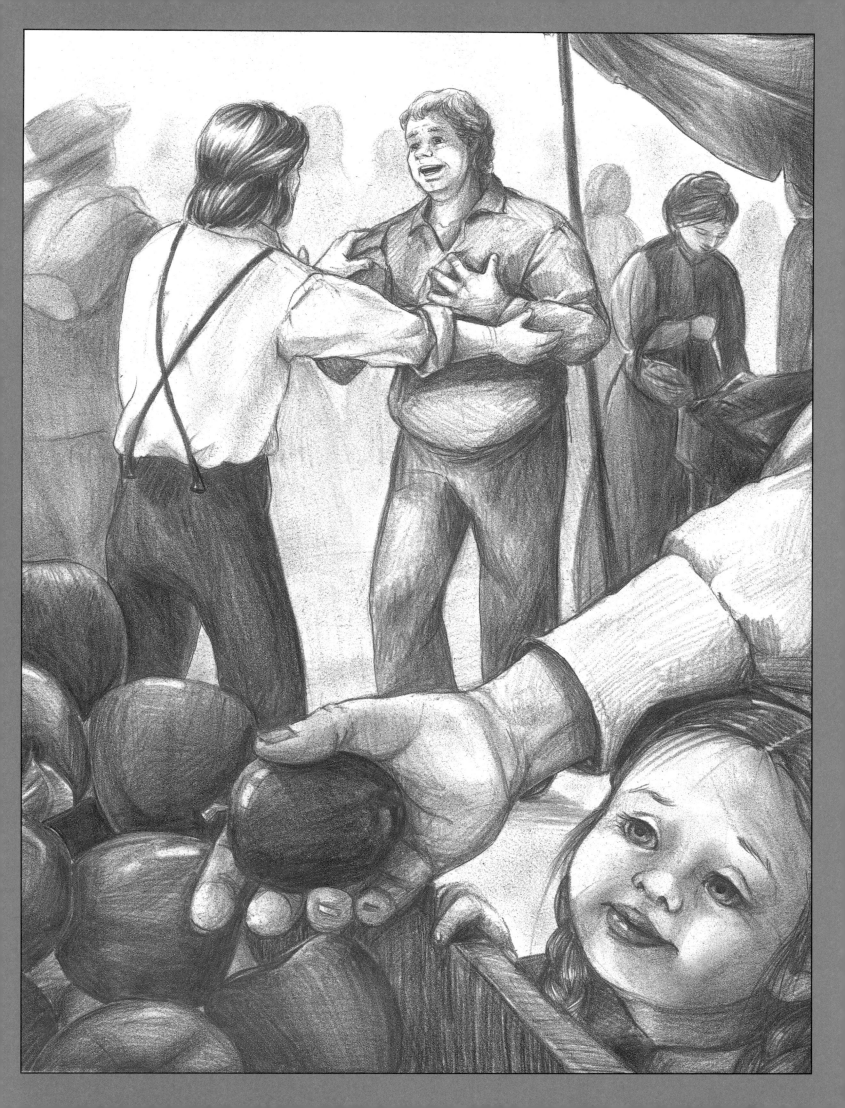

Mr. and Mrs. Kendrick invited Casper into their home to stay until he could build a home of his own. Mrs. Kendrick taught Casper how to speak English, and Mr. Kendrick helped him find a job cutting stone. Casper sent much of his earnings back to Catherine so that she and their children could join him one day.

Soon Casper was building a cabin in the hills of Greene County in Taylor Township and making furniture for his family.

One day in 1850 a man came to Casper while he was cutting stone to tell him that a family had arrived in the valley. Word had come that they needed someone who could speak their language, German. Casper set down his tools. "Maybe this family will have a letter from Catherine," he thought as he quickly rode to the valley. When he arrived, instead of a family of strangers, he found Catherine, accompanied by seven—not six—children. She had given birth to twins, a girl and a boy. There were hugs for everyone as Casper met his new children, Caroline and Charles.

Somehow, Catherine's letters telling Casper of the twins' births and that the family was coming to America had not reached him. She had used the money Casper had sent to her along with money from the sale of the farm in Switzerland to bring the family across the sea much sooner than they had thought possible. Casper soon learned that Catherine and the children had experienced some exciting adventures of their own.

AFTER THE TWINS' BIRTHS, Catherine and the children moved to Hamburg to await their chance to sail to America. They were befriended there by a nursemaid who helped care for the babies. However, the nursemaid became very attached to the baby boy, Charles. When Catherine and the children reached the dock, ready to board the ship, the nursemaid refused to give Charles to his mother. Catherine snatched the child from the nursemaid and ran up the plank to join the rest of her children just moments before the ship sailed away.

Like her husband, Catherine possessed the spirit of a pioneer. She and Elizabeth, Louisa, Rudolph, Mary, Ferdinand, Caroline, and Charles traveled by ship across the Atlantic Ocean to New York City and by stagecoach from New York to Philadelphia, Pennsylvania, and from Philadelphia to Pittsburgh, Pennsylvania. At Pittsburgh, they boarded a flatboat that took them down the Ohio River to New Albany, Indiana. Here they rented an ox and a covered wagon to travel to Greene County in southwestern Indiana—their new American home.

Together again, the family began life in a new country, planting crops, raising cattle, and enjoying their new-found freedom. The Hasler family grew as new twins, John and Roseanna, were born, followed by Edward, William, and Arnold. For Casper and Catherine, nothing meant more than watching their children grow up in their adopted land, America.

"Well, Hugh, that's the story that has been passed down from generation to generation—from Casper to Charles, from Charles to Jasper, from Jasper to your grandfather, Kenneth, from Kenneth to me, and now from me to you," said Hugh's dad.

"Wow, I can't wait to tell the kids at school!" Hugh said excitedly. "Sailing ships, stagecoaches, riverboats, and covered wagons. Charles and that bad nursemaid. And all those kids in one family? What a story!"

"Yes, Hugh," his dad said. "And the best part is—it's *our* story."

Charles & Jasper

Casper & Charles

Jasper & Kenneth

Brian & Hugh

Kenneth & Brian

Afterword
Researching Family History

WHAT A BRAVE ADVENTURE the Hasler family had! As exciting as their story is, however, it is not uncommon. All Americans moved here from someplace else. Native-American ancestors immigrated thousands of years ago. Europeans came to stay after Columbus reached America in 1492. Merchants wanted to trade products with Native Americans. Settlers like the Haslers hoped to build wealthier and freer lives here than they could in their homelands. Some settlers brought slaves from Africa to work vast farms called plantations. After the United States became a nation, people from all over the world moved here. Each immigrant experienced adventures as he or she moved away from home *forever*, undertook the long, dangerous journey, and built a new life in America.

Reading the Haslers' immigration story might make you wonder how your family came to America. Where did they live before they came here? Why did they decide to come? How did they travel here? What was it like to be a new American? If your parents have never mentioned stories about how their families came to America, you might ask them if they know. If they don't, your aunts, uncles, or grandparents might know. If your family includes stepparents, foster parents, or adopted parents, learn about their stories. After all, *they are your family*. Besides, as Americans, we all share the tradition of moving here from another country. In important ways, each immigration story is our story, too!

After you hear a story (or two) about how your family came to America, you might wonder if it is all true. Some parts of it may sound amazing—like the part of the Haslers' story in which Catherine brings seven children, including two babies, to Indiana by herself. Could she really have done that? How would you find out if it was true or not? What if you wanted to know more about what happened to Casper and Catherine and their children in Indiana? Where would you look?

People who collect their family stories, try to discover if they are true, and find more facts about their ancestors are called genealogists (gee-nee-*ol*-o-jists) or family historians. Family historians are like detectives, searching out clues about people who lived long ago. They do much of their detective work in libraries, especially libraries that own old books, such as county histories, and documents, such as government records, letters, and diaries. Many public libraries collect documents like these from their town or county. They can help you find your ancestors, prove that they really lived, and tell you a few details about their lives.

Charles and Malissa (Mullis) Hasler. Hasler family historians state that this photograph was taken on Charles and Malissa's wedding day, which, according to Greene County marriage records, was September 7, 1871.

But there are so many kinds of documents! How will you know where to start? Genealogists start their search in census records and vital records. **Census records** are created by U.S. government officials every ten years, when they count all the people who live in each household, and record their names, ages, and other facts about them. **Vital records** are the documents that tell us about when a person was born, when he or she was married and had children, and when the individual died. You can often find information about census and vital records in your public library and sometimes on the Internet.

Let's see what census records tell us about the Haslers. This family first appears in the Greene County, Indiana, census in 1850, as we would expect from reading the story. As sometimes happens in old records, Casper's name is spelled differently as "Jasper," his age is given as 37, and his occupation or work as stonemason. His household includes: Katherine, 35 years

```
754 HASLER    Jasper      37          M        Stonemason 500      SWIZ
              Katherine   35          F                            SWIZ
              Elizabeth   13          F                            SWIZ
              Louisa      11          F                            SWIZ
              Rudolph      9          M                            SWIZ
              Mary         8          F                            SWIZ
              Ferdinand    6          M                            SWIZ
              Caroline   9mo.         F                            SWIZ
              Charles    9mo.         M                            SWIZ
```

*1850 U.S. census data for the "Jasper" and "Katherine" Hasler household,
from* 1850 Census of Greene County, Indiana, *compiled by Mary Lou Wiles
(Bloomington, Ind.: Professor Copiers, [1985?], 222)*

old; Elizabeth, 13; Louisa, 11; Rudolph, 9; Mary, 8; Ferdinand, 6; and Caroline and Charles, 9 months. They were all born in Switzerland. The 1860 census shows us the children who were born in Indiana: John and Rose A., the new twins, were 8; Edward was 7, and William was 1. Arnold is missing, but having found the rest of the children, it is easy to imagine that Arnold was born after 1860.

The census and vital records tell us other interesting facts about the Hasler family as well. For instance, the 1860 census presents a mystery. Elizabeth is no longer listed, but there is a boy named Benjamin B*oo*mer, born in 1859, living with the Haslers. Where did Elizabeth go? Who is Benjamin? Maybe the vital records can tell us. Since the government did not keep birth records before 1882, we will start with marriage records. These records state that Elizabeth married a man named Elias B*au*man on July 8, 1858. If Benjamin's name was misspelled on the census records, he may be their son. Elizabeth and Elias are not listed in the 1860 census, nor are there any death records for them. What happened to them? Do they have a connection to Benjamin? Let's check the records for Benjamin to see.

The marriage records show that Benjamin B*oo*man (B*au*man?) was married in 1883 and that his parents were Elizabeth and Elias. The 1880 census lists Benjamin, born in 1859, as a son in the home of Casper and Catherine Hasler. Apparently they raised him. Why? The census and vital records do not say. However, Hasler family historians believe that Elizabeth died in 1859, giving birth to Benjamin and another infant—a

Marriage license for Elias and Elizabeth (Hasler) Bauman, dated July 8, 1858, from the Greene County marriage records

twin. After reading the information in the census and vital records, it is easy but sad to think that Elizabeth died in childbirth and that the Haslers raised their grandson. After all, their family story tells us how important each child was to this family! They might have raised Benjamin, their eldest daughter's son, as their own. Only more research would tell us for sure.

What fun and mysterious information do you suppose the census and vital records can tell you about your family? Visit your public library or log on to the Internet and search for census records, birth records, marriage records, and death records to see. Happy hunting!

M. TERESA BAER
Indiana Historical Society, Family History Publications

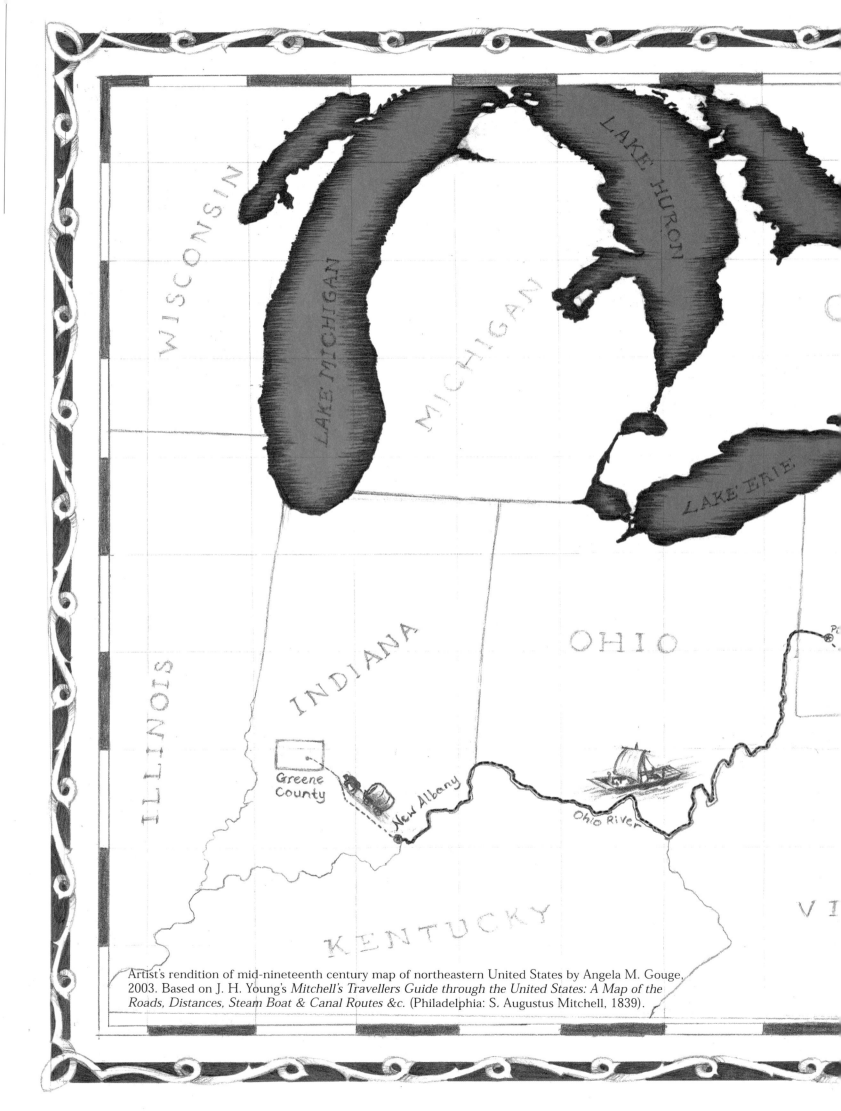

Artist's rendition of mid-nineteenth century map of northeastern United States by Angela M. Gouge, 2003. Based on J. H. Young's *Mitchell's Travellers Guide through the United States: A Map of the Roads, Distances, Steam Boat & Canal Routes &c.* (Philadelphia: S. Augustus Mitchell, 1839).